Thank You Notes to Max Fallek

*Thank you much for the time you spent visiting me
while I was in the hospital. Your prayers of healing
and your words of support made me fell such comfort.
I am convinced that your prayers with me, before my
endoscopic exam gave me the strength that I didn't
think I had. I loved the beautiful cards you brought from
the Sunday School and they brightened up my spirits
each day.*

– T. C.

*We want to thank you so much for all your visits to Gene
in the hospital over these last few years. He was always
touched by your visits. We are also very grateful to you
for being there to comfort us during such a difficult time
in our lives. Your compassion and thoughtfulness will
never be forgotten.*

– J. W.

*I don't have the words to express my gratitude for your
support of Howard Efron and I during his illness. Your
visits were always welcomed by both of us. Your words
and presence were comforting. Thank you for the poem
Howard requested be passed along and for the Kirby
Puckett picture. Your guidance of my family at the
memorial service was also appreciated.*

– L. L.

*How can we thank you enough for your loving kindness
in your visits with our Howard. Your payers and calm
demeanor were a comfort to all of us.*

– H. E. and family

*...A special thanks to Chaplain Max Fallek for his
friendship, love and support. It's a great feeling
physically and spiritually to have a Rebi making the
Meseberach for your health. My husband and I were
deeply touched by his prayers which occurred every
single day. Thank you Rebi Fallek for your compassion
and help which gave me strength and the will to live.*

– K. Y.

*...Max Fallek is one special person representing the
Spiritual Care Department. He came to us-honestly as an
angel to pray with us-when things were so bad-turned out
swell-turned out all of you are very special.*

– A. D.

*I am finally feeling well enough to formally thank you for
all your kindness while I was hospitalized at Methodist.
I greatly appreciated your comforting words, prayers,
Temple Israel cards, "Hannuka Harry" stuffed animal
(dog) and the menorah that you placed in my hospital
room. Your thoughtfulness lifted my spirits. Your caring
makes an important difference to those who are ill and in
need. I will always be grateful that you were there for me.
Be well!*

– J. M.

Touching
the Soul

The Diary of a
Jewish Chaplin

NODIN PRESS

Second printing, revised, 2016

design: John Toren

ISBN 978-1-932472-77-6

Library of Congress Control Number: 2008930902

Nodin Press, LLC
5114 Cedar Lake Road
Minneapolis, MN
55416

To my wife Lillian and our family,

David and Fumiyo, Susan and Keith,

who are traveling with me

on my life's journey

Bill,
THANk you FoR BEiNG
PART oF my JouRWEY
BoTh iN hitLe & Rh-Ball

Mck Fredd
9-7-'16

Contents

Acknowledgements

Alvin Fine says of life, "it is a journey, a going—a growing from stage to stage." I could say the same thing about compiling this diary. I have been profoundly moved by the many patients I have visited in hospitals and hospices as a Jewish chaplain. Each visit was very special, and many patients have heartwarming stories to tell. Eventually it occurred to me that I ought to share these stories with others, and I began to write this book. I wish to thank all the wonderful people who have inspired me along the way.

I am deeply grateful to Rabbi Max A. Shapiro, Rabbi Emeritus of Temple Israel of Minneapolis, who has been my religious and spiritual mentor for more than fifty years. With his encouragement I have been passionately involved in Social Action, humbly hoping that it has eased some of the pain and suffering of those less fortunate in our midst.

Rabbi Marcia Zimmerman, Senior Rabbi of Temple Israel, has been a constant source of support, suggesting that I begin visiting Temple Israel congregants during their hospital stay. As an outgrowth of these visits I was instrumental in forming the Benei Nu committee with an emphasis on Bikur Cholim (visiting the sick). This framed my chaplaincy foundation.

Each of the vignettes in *Touching the Soul: Diary of a Jewish Chaplain* carries a Yiddish title. Although my parents often spoke in Yiddish, rarely did I ever see the Yiddish language in writing. I had the opportunity to make the acquaintance of Philip Kutner, known throughout the Yiddish world as Fishl. He is considered one of the foremost Yiddish exponents in the United States. As editor and publisher of *Der Bay*, Fishl promotes both spoken and written Yiddish. He has been a guide, mentor and friend to me in the writing of this book—indeed, a *mentsh* by every meaning of the word.

I owe much to the Spiritual Care Departments at the Minneapolis Veterans Home under the leadership of Chaplains Neil Herring and Shelly Dugan, and the two directors of the Spiritual Care Department at Park Nicollet Methodist Hospital, David Berg and Scott McRae. Many thanks go to the Clergy Staff at Temple Israel including Rabbis Simeon Glaser and Jared Saks and Cantor Barry Abelson, who were always available to answer my many questions on Jewish ritual, history and customs.

I am grateful to my friend Stuart Fogel whose artistic cartoon renditions accompany some of the stories. He truly captures the essence of their Yiddishkeit flavor. I cannot thank my wife Lillian enough. She has been a constant and positive source of support in my own life's struggles and has always been understanding when I was called upon in a special situation, be it an urgent hospital visit or making myself available for a Shiva or funeral service.

Finally, I have been inspired by witnessing the struggles of my own children. As my daughter Susan and son David have said, they are most proud of my calling and have directed their own lives to being supportive to those in need.

I feel blessed to have had the opportunity to meet so many beautiful people and, in some small way, they have been a source of consolation and comfort, even joy, at their most difficult and often sad time. For it has been a "journey, a going—a growing from stage to stage."

Introduction

The Talmud teaches us: "to save one soul is to save the world." The saving of the soul is not simply the saving of a human life. Nor is it only the saving of a fellow human from bodily harm or a life threatening sickness. Rather, there are many ways that a soul can be saved. For example:

- Providing aid and comfort to one who is under physical or emotional pain.
- Listening to an individual who is in the last stages of his or her life.
- Giving support to family members and friends.
- Just being present when one is under duress.
- Adding a little humor to break the solemnity of the situation.
- Seeing that a much-wanted desire comes to fruition.

For the past several years, I have been blessed with the opportunity to serve as a Jewish hospital chaplain, doing *Bikur Cholim*—visiting the sick. Each visit has been unique because each and every patient I have visited has a distinctive personality, and during many of these visits I have "saved a soul" in each of the ways described above.

Over the years I have recorded incidents from many such visits in a journal. Since these visits have been primarily with Jewish patients, these notes have naturally taken on a Jewish flavor. This Jewish flavor is indeed unique and does not always appeal to my non-Jewish colleagues.

Of course, Judaism is not limited to a theological derivation or a belief in God. It encompasses a much broader base which includes culture, food, music and humor. My visits almost always include the playing of "Jewish Geography"—a game by which the patient and I uncover who we both know, whether it be a Jewish friend, a relative, business associate or neighbor. Finally, Jewishness includes a second common language—Yiddish.

Yiddish, to us Jews, is our *Mama-Loshen* or mother tongue. It is the language our grandparents spoke in their native European land, and kept alive even after they immigrated to America, in neighborhoods on the East Side of New York, the North Side of Chicago, and the North Side of Minneapolis. It is the language passed on down to our parents and often picked up by members of my own generation.

Leo Rosten, the noted Yiddish authority, states that "Yiddish illustrates how a beautiful language reflects the variety of life itself and in the special culture of Jews with their distinctive style of thoughts and subtleties of feeling."

Thus, with the countless hundreds of bedside calls I have made, I doubt if I ever had a patient not smile when I said on leaving, "*Zeigezunt*"—meaning "Be well," or "*Gezunterhait*"—"Good health to you." Often the patient would quickly respond to me by saying, "*Alevei*" —"it should happen to me."

In the following pages I describe a number of my visits with patients. Some are sad, others happy; the feelings they express range from remorse and regret to joy and thankfulness. Each visit reflects an important stage of that person's life. It is with this in mind that I have given each of my stories a Yiddish title. For only by using "Mama-Loshen" can I give special significance to each individual that I write about.

Paul Kriwaczek, in his book *Yiddish Civilisation*, says, "the adoption of Yiddish ancestry, language, mores and customs does serve as a social bridge. It provides a unifying force to marry the disparate sectors of the Jewish world: the ultra-orthodox, the Chassidim, conservative, reform, and liberal Jews, and agnostics and atheists of "Jewish origin." Thus the Yiddish Language is often interwoven with being Jewish. It is our "Mama Loshen."

(Note: Spelling standards for the Yiddish language have been set by **YIVO,** formerly the **Yiddish Scientific Institute** of Vilna, Poland. Now headquartered in New York, it has been renamed **YIVO Institute for Jewish Research** and is dedicated to the history and culture of Ashkenazi Jewry, which includes the

Yiddish language. This book, however, is written for the lay person, whether he or she is Jewish or Christian, sectarian or non-sectarian. Thus, I have chosen a spelling for each Yiddish word based on the phonetic or sound of the word rather then the official Yiddish spelling as set forth by **YIVO.)**

A Shaineh Maidel

O ne of my favorite expressions, especially in a time of distress, is "let's make lemonade out of lemons." The opportunity for using this expression often presents itself when visiting people either in a hospital or nursing home, when they are often quite discouraged, sometimes almost to the point of despair.

Such was the case with Pearl, whose husband Joseph, in his mid eighties, had been admitted to a nursing home. Joseph had been a model citizen in his community. Highly successful in his business, he participated in a wide variety of civic activities, both Jewish and non-Jewish. Joseph and Pearl enjoyed fifty-five years together which she described to me as "a match made in heaven."

Eighteen months earlier, Joseph had been diagnosed with the early stages of Alzheimer's. Shortly thereafter, his condition began to go downhill. As his condition worsened, and he began to wander off, Pearl became concerned that he would harm himself, and eventually found it necessary to place Joseph in a nursing home. It was a non-sectarian home, and upon receiving a call from the Chaplain, I made my first visit with them both. Prior to seeing him, I had met alone with Pearl. She told me she was quite discouraged with Joseph's condition. For the past two months, she had had no conversation with her husband. How discouraging it was.

She shared with me the beautiful relationship the two had enjoyed not only during their fifty-five years of matrimony, but from the first moment they met. Now however, being with her husband was like being with a "non-persona" since he would no longer communicate with her, regardless of the subject at hand. In other words, both his short and long term memory did not respond.

This was confirmed on my initial meeting with Joseph. I tried to bring him into a conversation, and Pearl kept saying, "See, I told you so. He just will not respond and he cannot respond."

I subsequently made a second appointment to see them both. Prior to the meeting I studied the notes I had taken at a workshop on working with people with dementia and Alzheimer. On seeing Pearl, I asked her to provide me with as much background as possible on Joseph's boy-

hood, his mother, his father, other family members, and most important, his own Jewishness and Jewish roots.

I then told her I would like to see how he would respond to a conversation about his childhood-held in Yiddish. As far as she knew, her husband had attended the Cheder (Jewish school) and was a Bar Mitzvah. In addition, he grew up in the Jewish immigrant area of North Minneapolis. Pearl said, "It will do no good, but if you feel that strongly about it, then try it."

On seeing Joseph, I asked him, "Joseph Vistache'du Yiddish?" He responded, "Vistache Yiddish." His eyes sparkled and he looked at me and said," "Vos macht du?" (What's new). As we carried on a conversation in his Yiddish and my half Yiddish-English his eyes sparkled. I noticed that Pearl's eyes swelled with tears of joy. I asked about his mother and father, his brothers and sisters. . . he talked about his childhood, his family Seders and how he found the Afikomen—even about his Bar Mitzva.

Then our conversation turned to Pearl. His short term memory was not there. But he recalled his early days with Pearl. I then looked straight into Joseph's eyes and asked him, "Who is the lady sitting next to me?" He looked at her and without hesitation said: "My shaineh maidel. Du bist mein shaineh maidel!" (You are my sweetheart.)

Pearl quickly hugged Joseph and said, "Oy azoy shain Harold." How beautiful Harold.

A Mitzva Gemacht in Gan Eiden

In his book *The Joys of Yiddish* Leo Rosten defines *Mitzva* as a "good work, truly virtuous kind, considerate, ethical deed." But how often one can say which *Mitzva* is more virtuous than another? But the rare occasion does arise in which one is able to give special meaning to a specific *Mitzva*. When that occurs, one can add the words "Gemacht in Gan Eiden," A "*Mitzva* made in Heaven."

Friday is always a special day since it is the beginning of our *Shabbes* or Sabbath. With this in mind, I have made it a point to drop by one of the hospitals to wish any patients I have seen during the week a *Shabbat Shalom* ... or "A peaceful and happy Sabbath."

On one such *Shabbat* visit I noticed a woman standing by the Chapel looking sad and in need of help. I introduced myself as a Jewish Chaplain at the hospital and asked her if there was anything I could do? After breaking down in tears she responded, "Yes, I am looking for a Chaplain. My mother is upstairs in the hospice with her boyfriend. She has less than a day or two to live. She has cancer and her last wish is for her and her boyfriend to be married before she dies."

I suggested that we have the hospital reception desk page for a Chaplain. She responded that a Chaplain had been paged a number of times with no response. Apparently, no other Chaplain was in the building. "What about you?" she asked, "Would you please marry my mother and her boyfriend?"

I went on to explain to her that I was a Jewish Chaplain, and not a Rabbi. In addition, from a legal standpoint I was not authorized to conduct a marriage ceremony. Further, since I was Jewish I would not be able to bless her mother and her mother's boyfriend in the traditional "Christian tradition." Then I added, "How would your mother and her boyfriend feel about having a Jewish Chaplain marry them?"

She responded by telling me, "This is of no consequence and what difference does it make? First of all, this is my mother's dying wish. Secondly, her boyfriend of over thirty years has only one concern: that she be happy and comfortable in her last day or two." Finally, the daughter looked at me and said: "Are we not all God's children? What difference does it make whether you are Catholic, Protestant, Buddhist or whatever. Would not the good Lord want my mother's dying wish to be carried out? And would not the Good Lord look upon you with joy?"

The look in my eyes gave away my answer. We immediately proceeded to her mother's bedside where her boyfriend was holding her hand. I was introduced as the Chaplain and from the grasp of our hands, I could tell she deeply appreciated my presence.

There we were, gathered all together. She with her intravenous feeding and morphine administering lines, her boyfriend, her daughter, and myself. The four of us engaged in conversation. She struggled to participate in a conversation with her nods of approval.

Without further ado, I proceeded with a make-shift ceremony, her mother and husband-to-be holding hands. As we proceeded through the ceremony, a glow came to her face, a smile broke through her pain and a look of serenity came into her eyes. I concluded with a "She-he-chi-anu," our traditional prayer of celebration reciting the Hebrew words of old:

Barukh Ahtah Adonai, Eloheynbu Melech Ha-Olam,
She-he-chi-anu, Vi-kee-iman, vi-hi-giano, la'zman
hazeh.

We praise You, Adonai Our God, Ruler of the Universe, who gives us life, sustains us, and enables us to share in wondrous occasions together.

On leaving the room her daughter said, "How can I thank you?" I simply responded, "No I am the one who should ask the question, how can I thank you for giving me the opportunity to do this Mitzva?" Truly, a "Mitzva Gemacht in Gan Eiden."

A Baseball Maivin

Nothing grips our country more during the month of October than World Series fever—the culminating clash of America's favorite sporting pastime. It starts with the playoffs in both the National and American Leagues and reaches a climax in the middle of the month with the final series itself. During this period, our eyes are glued to the television night after night as we watch our hometown or adopted team. Each morning we rush to read the quotations and comments of our favorite players in the daily newspaper.

Such was the case with Howard. He was a very young man of only fifty-two years. I met Howard on one of my hospital visits. He had been admitted for treatment of a lymphoma centered in his jaw. I had the opportunity to see him during each of several hospital admissions. At our very first meeting I also met his loving wife, Connie, who was always at his side giving him encouragement and support. His father and I knew each other from the local sports and health club.

Early on, Howard recognized that he was terminally ill. Despite this, he was always upbeat and maintained a positive attitude toward both his own life and that of others. There was not one ounce of bitterness in his thoughts, his deeds, or his words. I could readily understand this once I had learned of Howard's own contributions as a stand-up comic for charity events, at senior citizen homes, and wherever smiles and laughter were needed.

When I came into his room during his last admittance, Howard was right up front with me. He said, "Max, there is nothing they can do for me this time, so I will most likely go into hospice. Connie and I both know this. You and I have talked about the soul and that there is a place beyond for me."

During the next three days I spent a number of hours getting to know both him and Connie. They had met several years earlier through a telephone dating service. They soon became inseparable and it was not long before they were married.

Howard's favorite hobby, aside from comedy, was baseball, and particularly the Minnesota Twins. He was a student of the game. He could quote facts, figures, teams and their players. Both baseball history and the latest scores were like second nature to him. As a child he had collected baseball cards and other baseball memorabilia. Connie quickly fell in love with the sport and this became one of their great joys in life. One of the highlights of their marriage was a visit to the famous Baseball Hall of Fame in Cooperstown, New York.

During our conversation, I asked Howard who his favorite baseball player was. It took him exactly no time at all to say "Kirby Puckett" with all of the strength that his cancer-wrecked body could muster. (As a matter of fact, Connie and he had attended Kirby's installation in baseball's Hall of Fame during their visit to Cooperstown.) No sooner had the words come out of his mouth, than the thought occurred to me: why not get an autographed picture of Kirby Puckett for him. However, this was late on a Monday afternoon and the Twins were preparing for their first playoff game with Oakland the very next day.

The next morning I called the Twins office and asked for Kirby Puckett's secretary. I told her of Howard's condition and what a wonderful caring gift it would be if she could arrange for an autographed picture of Kirby with a message addressed to Howard. Later that afternoon, during my visit with Howard, I told him that I was going to the game that evening and I would bring him a memento. I imagined it would be a Homer Hankie, since I had not heard from the Twins office, but much to my surprise, on arriving at the office Wednesday morning there was a message inviting me to to come down to the Twins executive office to pick up my picture.

Late that morning I returned to Howard's room with the picture in hand. He was sitting up on his bed. He greeted me by saying, "Max, our Twins won last night and we are up one game.

Did you bring me a souvenir from the game?"

I said to Howard: "Who did you tell me was your favorite Minnesota Twins player?"

"Kirby Puckett," was his reply. I then handed him an envelope. When he pulled out the picture, his eyes popped wide open and he said: "Oh my God, oh my God. It is from Kirby Puckett, and he has addressed it to me—Dear Howard." Connie, who had been out of the room, entered, and he said, "Would you believe it, Connie, look what I have?" They embraced and both of them began to cry.

On Friday Howard's condition worsened. Connie had placed Kirby's picture on a shelf facing her husband. By that evening he was in a deep coma. Connie called early Saturday morning to let me know the end was near. I immediately went to the hospital where Connie, her sister and brother, and Howard's Dad were holding vigil with Howard. He died at 10:21 that morning.

The last item Connie removed from the room was the picture of Kirby Puckett watching over Howard. Truly, "A baseball maivin."

Mein Kinder

Nothing is more touching in life then the love of a mother for her children. Our immigrant grandparents would often refer to their children in Yiddish as "mein kinder." An old Spanish proverb says, *Amor de grande, amor de madre.* "A mother's love is a great love."

Such was the case with Myra. Forty-five years of age, Myra was a young mother in the prime of her life. A heavy smoker since she was nine years old, Myra left home during her impressionistic teenage years and found her way to Minneapolis. Struggling to find herself, she became involved with the local hippies and experimented with various drugs and life-styles. At the age of thirty-two she rediscovered herself and met her husband to be, who was non-Jewish. They married and settled down in a small town in northern Minnesota. Her husband, who suffered from a mental illness, was in and out of work throughout their married life. They had two children, a son and a daughter. Throughout her marriage, she maintained a "Jewish home." She celebrated the holidays in her own way and bestowed the meaning of being Jewish on her two children. Myra came down with lung cancer and within six months, after having tried both chemotherapy and radiation, she went into a hospice at Park Nicollet Methodist Hospital.

Shortly after coming down with her illness, Myra and her husband agreed that it would be best if the children went to live with their *Bubbie* (grandmother) in Florida. So it was, and the children bade farewell to their mother. Their father promised to visit them several times each year.

On visiting with Myra during her last days, I asked her if there was anything I could do for her. She said to me, "I understand that being Jewish means that I cannot be cremated but I want very much to be cremated. What can you do about this?" She went on to say, "This is very important to me. Please do what you can do about arranging for this!"

I explained to her that in our Jewish tradition, burial of the entire body is preferred since as the Torah teaches us, "We leave the world in the same way as we come into it." This being as a whole body. There is also a second reason for the Jewish view towards cremation—the Holocaust. Cremation reminds us too much of what took place during that horrific period.

However, the Reform movement does take a different view towards cremation. Accordingly, cremation does take place, although not all Reform rabbis will officiate at a service for one who has been cremated. On discussing this further, her husband and I assured her that cremation would be arranged.

Being of the inquisitive mind, I asked Myra if she would share with me why being cremated was so very important to her. This is what she told me in a feint whispering voice,

"My children who are nine and six live with my mother in Daytona. Right now during the summer, almost every day *Bubbie* takes them to a nearby beach for a swim. Even when school starts, they will still go swimming on weekends. After I am cremated, I want my ashes spread in the Atlantic Ocean off of that Daytona beach where my children swim. In this way, I can be ever so close to "mein kinder."

What more is there to say? "Mein Kinder."

Alevei

Everyone should have the *mazel* (good fortune) to experience *Alevei*. It is an age-old Yiddish expression meaning, "It should happen to me or happen to you!" Or, as some people say: "Alevei, please God!"

Sandra, a young seventy-year-old, was admitted into the hospital with an uneven heart beat. She had received a quadruple bypass a number of years earlier and a pacemaker two years later. Yet she continued to have difficulty with her uneven heart beat. Each time she experienced this condition, she was rushed to the hospital cardiac unit for diagnosis and treatment.

The prescribed treatment is called an "electrical cardioversion." Here the upper chamber of the heart is treated for "atrial fibrillation" by subjecting the patient to electrical impulses brought to the heart by applying the paddles from the same equipment used to restore a heartbeat during cardiac arrest. The procedure is considered quite safe but patients often experience extreme anxiety, not surprisingly. This is because they often fear any type of electrical shock stimulation since they equate it with cardiac arrest.

The moment I walked into her room, I could tell that such was the case with Sandra. When I introduced myself she immediately said, "Oh Max, I have heard about you. Two of my neighbors, Mary Strauss and Doris Horowitz, mentioned your name to me."

Sandra described to me her current heart condition and shared with me how extremely anxious she was about the electrical cardioversion treatment she was to undergo later that afternoon. I could see she was quite pale and extremely nervous. She did not hesitate to tell me how frightened she was and even expressed fear that she would not pull through. I then offered to say a "Mi Sheberach" (healing prayer) for her, which she immediately accepted.

Taking both of her hands I began the prayer. I could feel her hands gripping my own ever so tightly. Her eyes opened and the tears began to flow. We continued to hold hands for several moments. Indeed it was a touching experience. In the prayer I asked that Sandra be given the strength to see her safely through her procedure. She immediately responded by saying, "Alevei, from your lips to God's ears!" After my farewell and good wishes I left the room.

The next morning when I came into her room there was Sandra, fully dressed, with a big smile on her face. She said, "I have two things to tell you. First, I am glad to see you, and secondly, I want to thank you. Did you hear what happened to me after you left the room yesterday?" I replied, "No, what happened?"

"Max, when you left the room, I got up to go to the bathroom and I kept saying to myself, Please, God, hear that prayer. I must have collapsed. The medical staff rushed in and thought I had gone into cardiac arrest. Instead, my heart beat had suddenly returned to normal, and the shock must have made me collapse. So I did not even have to go through that electrical treatment. Something in your prayer must have clicked!"

Sandra went on to say: "Alevei, Alevei!"

Azoiner Malach

There is nothing in the world more tragic then the death of a child. No matter how long one lives or what one does, it is something that stays with the person throughout his or her lifetime.

I have been most fortunate not to experience very many hospital calls, or to have been called upon to lead a Shiva Service where a child has passed away, regardless of the age. While I was in grade school, I lost two teenage friends. Their loss has always stayed with me. There is little one can say or one can do when there is a loss of a child. Thus, often in our Jewish faith, we turn to the Rabbis of old, or stories that have been handed down to us either from an unknown author or one who is known.

Such was the case with a couple I met at one of our Minneapolis hospitals. They had lost a young daughter. For the next year each and every time I saw them, they reminded me of their beloved Esther who had been taken from them too soon. We would sit and talk and even though they had two other children, they would only talk about their beloved Esther. On one such occasion, I asked if I could share with them a story that Rabbi Daniel B. Syme, formerly with the Union of American Hebrew Congregations, had shared with his audience during a talk he gave on the Jewish meaning of death.

The story went like this. Legend has it that

there was a man living in eastern Poland who lost his wife at a very early age. A push cart peddler by trade, he was left with two small children, a son and a daughter. He watched over them, cared for them and nourished them. Soon afterwards his daughter too got sick and died. He was both sad and angry. He asked God, "How can the God I believe in take both my wife and daughter at such an age? What kind of God are you? How could you do this to me? The God that I have always believed in! A God is supposed to be just and fair!"

He became very morbid. He sat at home and forgot about his own business and started to ignore his son. He kept alternating between anger and sadness. Then one night he had a dream. He dreamed a procession of angels were marching down from heaven. Each angel was holding a lighted candle. As they passed by him, he noticed that at the very end of the procession was his daughter.

As his daughter passed him, she too, was carrying a candle, but her candle was unlit. He looked at her and then asked, "Daughter, tell me, why is it that all the other angels are carrying lighted candles, but yours is unlit?" She looked at him and said, "Daddy, every time the angels light my candle, your tears keep putting it out!"

I did not see the couple for a few years. Then, as in the past, our paths crossed once again. Their first comment to me was in ques-

tion form: "How is your wife and family?"
Then they told me about their own remaining
children. They where growing and brought
them such joy! Then they concluded by saying, "Max, we often think of our angel and
what she wants us to do!"

Azoiner Malach. Such an angel.

A Gut Neshome

I truly have been blessed in making hospital
calls over the past several years. Each and
every visit has had its own special set of rewards.
These rewards reveal themselves in the comfort
and solace gained by the person I am visiting
or his or her family and friends. They run the
full gamut of emotions from sadness to depression, from happiness to joy, and from anger to
peacefulness.

They may take the form of a simple smile or a hearty laughter, a single tear or a flow of tears, the squeeze of a hand or a warm and tender embrace. Regardless of the depth of feeling or the change in physical expression I receive from a patient, such rewards often come right at the time of my visit. But every once in awhile, the reward comes at a much later date.

Such was the case with Harold, now in his eighties. Harold was a resident in the Minneapolis Veterans Home. In fact he was the first Veterans Home resident I visited. On our first meeting, I found Harold racing around the corridors of the Home in his wheelchair going from one floor to another. His vivaciousness and daily greetings brought smiles and cheered residents and staff alike.

Harold was a wonderful artist, and spent a good deal of his time doing various arts and crafts. No project was too difficult—Harold always rose to the challenge. So good was his work that in 1998 he won first place in a National Arts and Crafts show for veteran nursing home residents sponsored by the U.S. Veterans Administration.

Harold was a World War II veteran, and he was proud of his U.S. Army service in the Pacific theater during World War II. But the most important part of Harold's life was his family. Pictures of his parents, his wife and brothers adorned the walls of his room, though pride of place went to the pictures of his son, daughter-in-law, and two grandsons. Whenever their names were mentioned, a broad smile came to his face.

I do not believe I have ever met anyone as proud of his or her Jewish heritage as Harold. Whenever there was a Jewish holiday, up on his walls and on top of his dresser would appear the symbols of the holiday. For example, a Menorah for Chanukah, a Seder plate for Passover, or a Happy Holiday greeting in English and Hebrew.

At each visit, I would bring him a delicacy from a local delicatessen. This might be apple strudel, a cheese Danish, or mandelbroit; corn beef, pastrami, chopped liver (or "Gehakte Leber" as he would call it) or matza ball or chicken noodle soup. We would break bread together, and always before the first bite, he would ask for the *Hamotzi* or prayer.

About four years after I met Harold he suffered a series of illnesses which left him unable to move around in his wheelchair or breathe without a tracheotomy tube. He was placed on intravenous feeding. At the same time, he lost his ability to speak. For the next several months, Harold communicated to me by writing notes, many of which were illegible. He could hear the questions I asked him, and he would respond with head nods, a smile, or the wave of his hand.

Harold's health continued to decline and he was moved to a local hospital. I made it a point to see him at least once every other week. One day before one of my visits, I had an opportunity to chat with my neighbor Bob Maisel, who happened to be an ear, nose and throat doctor. I told him about Harold and asked him, "Why is it that I often hear people with a tracheotomy being able to speak, yet, Harold is unable to do so." Bob mentioned that Harold might possibly have had some other complication. He said, "Max, why don't you speak with his doctor?"

On my next visit with Harold, I sent a note to his doctor. Two weeks later, on my next visit, I found the doctor had left me a note simply saying that if Harold wanted to speak, ask the nurse to hook him up with a tracheotomy mask. One of the nurses did this, and would you believe, Harold could talk. Not in long conversation but enough to bring a smile to his face, because once again he could verbally express his needs and feelings. I immediately communicated this discovery to his son David. One can only imagine his joy on being able to carry on a conversation with his father. On the other hand, I was at a loss for words to describe my own feelings of fulfillment and happiness. Drops came to my eyes when David said to me, "You are a *Gut Neshome*—a good soul."

Bashert

M aking the rounds in a hospital gives a Jewish Chaplain many opportunities to play the game of Jewish Geography. This often leads one to say: "It's *bashert*." What a wonderful expression in the Yiddish language. Who has not experienced the meaning of this expression? For it means, "It is meant to be."

On one such occasion I walked into room 546 to visit Elsie Golden. A wonderful woman no more than five feet tall, she was in her late seventies when she was brought into the hospital to undergo surgery for an advanced stage of colon cancer. At her bedside was her daughter June, a woman of fifty-two years of age. Taking Elsie's hand, I introduced myself as the hospital's Jewish Chaplain. She was quite weak, yet had a beautiful smile on her face.

Her daughter June just stared at me. Then she uttered, "Max Fallek! Are you Max Fallek? Don't you know who I am?" I looked and said, "June! June Golden? No, it cannot be. My God, it's *bashert*."

To explain this happening, I must go back fifty years, to 1957, when I moved to Minneapolis on completing my naval duty following the Korean War. I had been offered a position with Minnesota Mining and Manufacturing Company in their Speech Writing Department. Hardly knowing anyone in the Twin Cities, I decided to see if there was a YMHA—now known as the Jewish Community Center—so I looked in the telephone book and came across the name of the Jewish Sheltering Home for Children.

I telephoned the home and spoke with its executive director, who told me that the facility served the needs of Jewish children placed there under either of two situations. Families in distress as a result of sickness or economic hardship could leave a child there temporarily. And the Jewish Family and Children's Service used the home for children waiting to find a suitable new home. The home was also known as the Oak Park Home for Children. Founded in the 1920's, it experienced its largest use during the Depression of the 1930's. Like many other orphanages and sheltering homes, its doors were closed in 1965 following a decline in the need for such organizations.

I will never forget my very first visit. There, Eve Goldfein, the Executive Director, welcomed me as if I was one of her own children. Mrs. Goldfein, or "Nana Goldfein," as the children addressed her, was a housemother's mother—warm, compassionate, understanding, and caring, yet firm when firmness was called for. Each and every child was treated as if he or she was Mrs. Goldfein's very own. The home itself soon became my "home away from home." She took me in as if I was one of her own children. Later, together with my wife Lillian and our children, David and Susan, we all were part of her family. Every weekend I would take one or more of the kids on an outing—to the zoo, to a movie, or to a sporting event or a park, just to mention a few places. One evening, the children and staff participated in the traditional Shabbat meal. Sometimes, following the meal, I took the older children to Shabbat Services at Temple Israel. Often, on Saturday mornings, I would take Joey, one of the boys who was studying for his Bar Mitzva, to the nearby Mikro Kodesh Conservative Synagogue for services.

On my first visit, I noticed there was one little five-year-old girl hiding behind a sofa. A true "Mazik" (full of mischief), she played this "hide-go-seek" game with me during the first three or four visits. Once she realized that I was returning every Saturday, this little girl—whose name, I soon learned, was June—warmed up to me. Thereafter, each and every time I came to the home she would rush up and jump into my arms.

Needless to say the grown woman standing next to me in Elsie Golden's hospital room was June.

June had been placed in the home because her own mother and father were unable to take care of her. Two years later she was placed in a foster home. Some time after that her mother and father regained custody of her. For forty-four years we had not seen one another. Yet here in room 546 we were reunited.

A few days later I found pictures of June I had taken when she lived at the Oak Park Home. Words cannot describe her feelings. She had never seen a picture of herself at the ages of five and six. The first words that came out of her mouth were, "My God, my own children looked like this at their age. Wait till they see these pictures!"

What more is there to say except for the words, "It's *bashert*."

Farblondzhet

How often does someone cross our path who has been truly nameless and faceless? A fellow human being, who for some reason hides his or her identity out of fear. Such was the case of Jack Rosen.

A World War II veteran, Jack had moved away from the Twin Cities following the war. Some forty years later he appeared out of nowhere at the intake desk at the Minneapolis Veterans Home. A spent and broken man, yet he was always friendly and was well liked by the other residents who made his acquaintance, and also by visitors and the staff.

It was a warm summer Friday evening. Upon returning with my wife from services at my own Temple Israel, I had an urgent message waiting on our telephone answering machine. It was from Pastor Neil Herring, the permanent

Chaplain at the Home. Would I please call him as soon as I got in, regardless of the hour?

After our usual greetings, Neil lost little time explaining his dilemma. "Max, I am so terribly embarrassed. We have a real problem here at the Home. Possibly there is someway you can help."

I said, "Whatever it is, I will do what I can." He proceeded to tell me a story, which at first was almost unbelievable.

Some fifteen years earlier, a Jack Rosen had been admitted to the Home. He had listed his religion on his registration and intake papers as "Catholic," and since that time it had been assumed that he *was* a Catholic.

He had passed away on the Wednesday of that week. No next of kin or relatives could be located. Thus, he was sent over to a local funeral home to be prepared for burial at the Fort Snelling National Cemetery. Late on Friday, the day I received the call, a relative was finally contacted. When told that the funeral would be Monday of the following week and that local priest would be available, the relative said: "What are you talking about? What do you mean, a Catholic priest? My uncle is Jewish and we want a Jewish funeral!"

Pastor Herring felt terribly embarrassed. What could he do? He went on to say that the body had already been embalmed, which is not in accordance with Jewish custom. I quickly responded: "Give me an hour and let's see what can be done. I first want to talk to our local Jewish funeral home, Hodroff and Sons, and see what they have to say.

"And by the way, Neil, " I added, "we have a Yiddish expression for something like this. The word is *Farbrondzhet* or "mixed-up."

A quick call to Hodroff and Sons was most settling. I was told not to worry about the cost or the arrangements. They would take care of everything. This they did. Obviously, the one question that still lingered was why Jack Rosen had identified himself as being a Catholic? On listening to the answer from the niece, my throat became dry and my heart ached.

According to the niece, Jack had often been

subjected to anti-Semitic remarks as he was growing up, and even during his time in the service. Thus when he was admitted to the Home, he wanted to make his life as peaceful as possible. In his mind, by not identifying himself as being Jewish he would accomplish this end.

Jack received his Jewish funeral with both friends and relatives in attendance. Some of the words with which I closed the service are still echoing in my mind:

At the rising of the sun and at its going down
We will remember him
At the blowing of the wind and in the chill of winter
We will remember him
At the opening of the buds and in the rebirth of spring
We will remember him

Upon conclusion of this recitation, Jack was afforded the customary twenty-one gun salute. He was truly at peace now.

And that is truly a *farblondzhet* story.

A Bisel Naches

S ometimes, *A Bisel Naches*, a little joy, turns into *A Fil Naches*, a lot of joy.

Marion and Irving as a couple could be role models for everyone. Both in their nineties, they had recently celebrated their sixty-sixth wedding anniversary. One could only marvel at their vitality, sense of humor, deep love and affection for one another, and their marvelous passion and zest for life. Although I had met this delightful couple a number of years ago, I got to know them on a more personal basis when I had the opportunity to visit Marion at the hospital when she was recovering from an illness.

We immediately took a liking toward one another. I remember so clearly, on my very first visit, that the blessing I offered for Marion's recovery set the stage for a long and lasting friendship. The first words out of her mouth when I offered the blessing were, "You mean you are going to say a special prayer for me? Why, that has never happened to me before!"

During our conversation, Jewish geography immediately came into play. We each could enumerate countless friends that we had in common. In addition, Marion and Irving had many relatives that had either crossed my path or that of my wife Lillian. This included nephews and nieces who were social acquaintances, those who served on boards of community agencies, and racquetball colleagues of mine.

Marion's stayed in the hospital for several days. During one of my visits, I got to meet her only daughter, who had come in from the East to be with her mother. On each and every day several friends or relatives came to visit. Unlike many of the other friendships which developed in the course of my hospital visits, our relationship continued and flourished after Marion returned home. Not only did our paths cross on numerous occasions, but in addition, we had a most unusual way of communicating with one another. We happened to have the same hair stylist. Thus, whenever Marion and her husband Irving had a hair appointment, they would leave a message for me. Likewise, when I went in for my haircut, I would leave a message for them with Laura, our stylist.

Several months after Marion's illness, we ran into one another at a Shiva (memorial) service for one of our mutual friends. Marion mentioned that she was going to give me a call on the following Monday. Two days later, she called and related the following to me. Irving was to celebrate his ninety-fifth birthday in two months. His great desire was to become a Bar Mitzvah since he had never studied or gone through the program in his youth. Marion's question to me was, "Max, can this be arranged in some way?" I told her, "Let me discuss this with the Rabbi and see what can be done."

My immediate thought was, Why not have Irving recite the prayers or blessings before and after the reading of the Torah and have him touch the Torah with the *Yad* or Torah-reading pointer. In this way, he would be performing activities similar to those performed by of a young boy of thirteen chanting his Bar Mitzvah Torah portion. I sent an email to the Rabbi asking her if something like this could be arranged. In no time flat, the Rabbi called Marion to inform her that both she and the Temple would be honored to do this for the family.

The Rabbi suggested that the event take place on the Friday evening of his ninety-fifth birthday week, when he would be given an *Aliya* (honor) by going through his Bar Mitzvah on the *Bimah* (pulpit) at that time. Marion immediately went to work to make the necessary arrangements. Invitations would be prepared. Family and friends would be invited.

What a glorious evening it turned out to be! At the appropriate time during the service, when the Torah was removed from the Ark, Irving and Marion were called to the *Bimah*. Irving recited his prayers beautifully. His Hebrew was flawless and he belted out a chant second to none.

The completion of his ceremony was greeted

with "Mazotofs." The Rabbi presented Irving with his Bar Mitzvah certificate and Marion gave him one of her patented kisses and embraces.

A happy and joyous *Oneg* (reception) was held for friends, relatives, and congregants at the conclusion of the service. Truely, *A Bisel Naches*—A Little Joy. Better still, *A Fil Naches*—Lots of Joy.

Oy, Vos a Mechaieh

Probably no Yiddish word has come up more often during my hospital visits than *mechaieh*. (Many readers may recognize the word as "m'-khy-eh.") It is truly one of our more beautiful and expressive Yiddish words. No word could have more onomatopoeia then *mechaieh*. Simply it means: "extreme pleasure" or "out of this world."

Beverly was born and raised in Queens, one of the five boroughs of New York. Raised in a traditional Jewish home, Beverly attended the University of Minnesota and received her degree in psychology. She met her husband Tom, a non-Jew, and they settled in western Minnesota where she became a family therapist working for her county welfare department.

After twenty-five years of a happy marriage, living without much Jewish contact, Beverly came down with a serious melanoma which rapidly metastasized. She was transferred to a Minneapolis hospital where she immediately underwent both chemo-therapy and radiation therapy, all of which was to no avail.

One day I received a call from the hospital chaplain office telling me that they had recently moved a patient into their hospice unit. Though the woman was unaffiliated, she was asking to see a Rabbi or a Jewish Chaplain. I immediately left for the hospital.

On coming into the room, I could see that Beverly was quite ill. I could tell that she probably had only a day or two at the most to live. Her coloring was very pallid. She could hardly speak. Her only sustenance was an IV. Beverly and I talked for close to an hour. At times, she was almost incoherent. Yet she was able to talk to me.

She told me about her childhood, her days on the streets of Brooklyn, Queens, and Manhattan, how she came to Minneapolis, and about life on the western prairie of Minnesota. The more we talked, the more she seemed to respond. It was like a transfusion.

We prayed together, we laughed and we cried together. I asked Beverly if there was anything I could do for her. She quickly responded with a firm, "Yes. My one last wish is to taste a *knish*. (Jewish dumpling filled with meat, potato or barley. Like a kalachi.) Without batting an eyelash, I told Beverly, "Just hold on, and I am going to grant you this wish."

It took me all of thirty minutes to go the Crossroads Delicatessen to order a knish. My friend Kevin, the co-owner, asked me what I wanted with one "knish"? When I told him about Beverly, he insisted that I take along three of them.

On returning to Beverly's room, I asked her nurse if it was all right for her to have a "knish." She said, "Listen, Beverly has not eaten any solids for three days, and I doubt if she will eat it. By all means you can try. It certainly will not hurt her."

I turned to Beverly and said, "I have a "knish" for you. In fact, I have three of them." I gave her tiny portions. She savored each and every morsel. It took her close to twenty minutes to eat one. Every little spoonful brought a smile to her face. Then she was finished. She looked at me and with tears rolling down her cheeks, she said, "Oy, vos a *mechaieh*." (What a pleasure)

Beverly died later that evening.

A Shaineh Mazik

A *shaineh mazik* is a mischievous girl or lady. The expression is almost always associated with one who is playfully joyous.

Alan Funt, creator of *Candid Camera*, was one of the first to develop the concept of "healing through laughter." Together with Norman Cousins, long time editor of the *Saturday Review of Literature*, he embarked on a nationwide public speaking tour fostering the idea.

Whenever I think of this concept, it brings to mind Dorothy Sterne. She was one of the most beautiful and positive women I have ever met. Everyone who knew Dorothy felt the same way about her. When she was diagnosed with breast cancer in her later seventies, she attacked her disease in the same spirit that she did everything else, using humor as her best medicine.

I always made it a point to see Dorothy both before and immediately after her chemotherapy treatment. Each and every visit concluded with Dorothy saying, regardless of who was in the room, "Max, it is now time for my prayer." I held Dorothy's hand and proceeded with our traditional prayer for healing:

Merciful God, we pray that Your healing presence will be close to Dorothy. Grant her renewed serenity and strength at this difficult time. Bless those who care for you, your doctors, nurses, care givers, your loving husband and children with added wisdom and patience. Help all those who pray for your healing to bear our burden of concern.

We praise you O God, Healer of the Sick
Baruch atah Adonoi rofay hacholim.

As Dorothy's illness became progressively worse, her commitment to live and to beat her illness increased proportionately. Her sense of humor seemed to grow with each and every passing week.

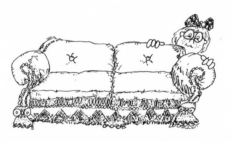

One day, while I was visiting with her, she asked me to sit on the edge of her bed since the only two chairs in the room were taken up with clothing. I sat and talked with her for the next twenty minutes.

Suddenly, there was a knock on the door. It was Roger, her husband. Roger came in and said, "Dorothy, I decided to come early and bring you a bagel and cream cheese nosh." She looked at her husband and quickly replied:

"Roger, why did you have to show up at this very minute. I finally get Max in bed with me and you have to come in with a farstunkene bagel."

Roger looked down at me with a smile and said, "Max-A bi gezunt"—you have better luck with her than I do." Dorothy was truly a "shaineh mazik."

Verstashe'du Yiddish

Arthur M. was truly a pillar of the Congregation. He was long active in our Temple. He became President of the congregation and immersed himself in Jewish and civic communal affairs. When I first arrived in Minneapolis, Arthur was one of the first Temple Israel congregants I met. We immediately took a liking to one another and he became a mentor to me in encouraging my participation at Temple Israel.

At the age of ninety-two, Arthur developed a number of medical problems consistent with his age. Besides having a severe heart problem, he had both uremic poisoning and liver failure. Once he was being hospitalized, he became a regular member of my hospital calling.

One afternoon I walked into his room and immediately discerned that he was not doing well. I said, "Arthur, is there anything I can do for you?"

"Yes, Max there is one thing you can do for me." he replied. "You see, I am going to die tonight. This I know. I don't think I have ever told you about my past. This I want to do. I was born in Germany and came to this country with my parents, settling in Chicago when I was five years old. We went to a traditional *shul* (synagogue) and much of the time my parents spoke only Yiddish.

"On attending school, I wanted to be as American as apple pie. Speak only English and do only what Americans do. Yet I wanted to preserve my Jewish identity which I was so proud of. Thus, I became attracted to the Reform Jewish movement, such as what it was at that time.

"I took a job as a traveling salesman for a furniture company and traveled Wisconsin, Minnesota, and the Dakotas. Minneapolis became my home. I met my wife Audrey there, also of a German Reform Jewish background. Her family and whose family was also active at Temple Israel.

"Like many of my fellow congregants, we dropped our Yiddish language in favor of speaking only in English. This was our way of assimilating and being looked upon by our Christian neighbors as "true Americans." And English is what I have been speaking day in and day out for the past eighty years."

At that point Arthur looked at me and said, "You know Max, my last wish is that you give me the opportunity to speak Yiddish with you." I looked down at Arthur and thought to myself, *God, how I wish my own mother and father had not covered up their own Yiddish by doing the same thing Arthur had done.* For when my parents did not want me to hear what they were saying, they spoke in Yiddish. Little did they realize I did understand a little.

I said, "Arthur, I verstashe Yiddish a bisel (little). I understand it more then I can speak it. *Zug mir* (tell me)." And *Zug mir* Arthur did. He talked on for forty minutes. We talked about foods including blintzes, latkes, matza ball or knaidelech soup, gefilte fish, bagels and biales.

Even chopped liver with smaltz.

Suddenly Arthur grew silent. He had the most wonderful smile on his face that I have ever seen. He looked up at me and said, "Max, please call my wife Audrey and tell her goodbye for me. Also say goodbye to your wife Lil for me. She is such a lady."

And with that Arthur closed his eyes. I said a *Shema* for him with a prayer for his peaceful journey and at the same time thanked God for the gifts that Arthur had given to me and to the world. I left the room. Arthur passed away that evening.

Borekh Hashe'm

L ike most active participants in *Bikur Cholim* (visiting the sick), I find that it brings solace and comfort to both family members and the one who is visited. More often than not, the visits are made with people who are unknown to me, or at the very most a casual acquaintance or friend. Although I feel that it is I who receives a gift as a result of every visit, it is truly special when I visit someone with whom I share a close family relationship. Such was the case with the story I am about to relate.

For the past several years I had met with several friends for breakfast every Saturday morning. During these meals we would chat, discuss the stock market, the Minnesota Gophers, Vikings, and Twins, and bring each other up to date on our family's activities during the previous week.

My friend Ron and his wife Rita have two children. Five years after graduating from college, his son Ben married, and within two years he and his wife Joan announced the pending birth of a son. Midway through Joan's pregnancy, it was discovered that their future son was missing a heart chamber. Needless to say, during Joan's entire pregnancy, the entire family was fearful of losing the child.

Extensive heart reconstruction surgery would be required, and the first stage was to occur within a week of the child's birth.

Jack, their son, came into this world on a lovely October day. He was immediately placed on a ventilator and a respirator, and was closely watched around the clock for five days, at which point the first of three planned surgeries was scheduled to take place.

The first stage of the three surgeries was devoted to constructing a new heart chamber. One cannot possibly describe the atmosphere of great fear and apprehension that pervaded the waiting room that day. Mother, father, both

Bubbies and the one *Zeide* (Grandmothers and Grandfather) were there as well as Jack's aunt, uncle, and close friends. There was hardly a word spoken. We all sat there looking so glum, so sad, and so worried. Hour after hour passed by. It seemed like an eternity.

I turned to everyone and said, "You know God is watching us all and at the same time he is watching over Jack. May I offer a prayer for his safety and for the success of his surgery?" The response was immediate: everyone stood and we held hands in a circle. I offered a prayer for Jack, his parents, his grandparents, and for those present, including his doctors, nurses, and care givers.

Upon the completion of the prayer, the ice was broken. There were tears, and there were smiles breaking through the tears. Would you believe that within ten minutes after our prayers, the head surgeon came to the waiting room to announce that Jack was going to be fine. He immediately huddled with Joan and Ben to review the finer details of the surgery. Shortly thereafter, they were allowed into the Intensive Care Recovery room to see Jack. *Borekh Hashe'm* (Thank God).

Ess Ess Gezunterheyt

The Talmud says "To Seek God is to be good. To find God is to do good." Such was the case with one of my very good friends. I met Bob shortly after I moved to Minneapolis following my tour in the United States Navy. Upon my arrival, I sought out a Jewish connection by looking at the Minneapolis telephone directory. I came across the Jewish Sheltering Home for Children, also known as the Oak Park Home for Jewish Children.

Founded in the early 1920's, the home sat on a lovely site in the heart of the then north side Jewish community. It was both a temporary shelter for children of families that ran into hard times and a haven for children who had lost their parents and were waiting for foster homes.

I was introduced to Bob and his family by the Home's house mother, who was a first cousin to his wife. We developed a close personal and business relationship. Bob was a very successful businessman, having started one of the first national temporary help firms. He grew up in Brooklyn where he met his wife, a Duluth, Minnesota, Minneapolis native. On moving to Minneapolis, he worked as an accountant before starting the business which made him nationally famous. However, he never forgot his roots. He was deeply proud of his Jewish roots, enjoyed talking in Yiddish, and made almost daily visits to a delicatessen.

In the late 1990's Bob's health began to fail. He was forced to give up driving. Thus, I would pick him up for a bi-weekly luncheon date. Needless to say, it would be to a local deli.

One spring day, Bob suffered a heart attack and was hospitalized.

I began making daily visits, and the two of us would talk and tell stories of the "good old days." But I could tell something was missing in Bob's hospital stay. Bob appeared to be very sad, even on the border of being depressed. I decided to delve into it further by asking him a series of questions. How did he like his hospital room? Did he have enough reading material? Was he being treated well? Was he hearing from his family? Did he have any regrets with about his life? Then, I asked him how he liked the food. Here, for the first time, he hesitated. He replied that it was fair, but unlike his other responses which were so spontaneous, his reply was a "feh" and a shrug of his shoulders. Something was obviously lacking.

After we said our goodbyes, I decided to bring something special to him. Upon receiving permission from his doctor, I brought both *gehochtah layber* (chopped liver) and a small bowl of *Knaiydlaech* (Matza ball) soup.

Words cannot describe the smile on Bob's face when he saw the small plate of chopped liver and the bowl of soup. His opening words were: "*Oy, alevei* (what good fortune)." He blurted out, "Max, how did you know?" We sat and ate together.

From that day on, I brought one or more traditional foods on every visit: kmish bread, chicken noodle soup, knishes, corn beef or pastrami, rugalah, even blintzes and smaltz herring. Prior to each of those eating sessions, Bob asked that we say the Hebrew blessing traditional with the breaking of bread:

*Baruch atoh adonoi hamotzi lechem min
haaretz*

*Praised be thou oh Lord our God, who brings
forth bread from the earth*

With that I simply said, "Bob, *ess ess gezunter-heyt* (eat, eat in good health)."

Mi Sheberach-Shiken Es Tsu Himl

A *Mi Sheberach* is a powerful Hebrew healing prayer. When this prayer is recited, our hope is that it will reach heaven. This is the story of a lady who, on hearing this prayer, said in Yiddish, "*Shiken es tsu himl*—Send it to heaven."

Sophie is ninety-five years young and wears her age as an optimistic young budding adult.

One could not be more beautiful at this age and indeed, more upbeat in her attitude and demeanor.

My very first visit with Sophie was a wonderful, warm, and inspiring session. I could not have asked for more. Our visit began with the usual introductions that I provided each patient. I identified myself as the Jewish Chaplain at the hospital and mentioned that at times I also represented the *Beinei Nu* (caring) committee at Temple Israel of Minneapolis. Before I could complete the introduction, Sophie made it abundantly clear that she was here only for what in the navy we called R and R: Rest and Rehabilitation.

She explained that hospitals were "not her thing." In her view chicken soup and "tender loving care" would and could go a lot further. After playing Jewish Geography and touching on mutual acquaintances, Sophie proceeded to tell me me how great life had been and how fortunate she had been to experience so much. This included both family and friends.

Towards the end of our conversation, I asked her if she wanted to have me say a prayer for her. She promptly replied, "Vhy not, It voud'nt hurt," in a semi Yiddish-English accent. So we proceeded to offer a *Mi Sheberach*, our traditional Healing Prayer. I then added my own personal touch, portions of which came from our conversation. Clasping Sophy's left hand with my own and touching her forehead with my right hand, I could see that her soul had been touched. Tears flowed from her sparkling eyes.

I was very moved. Upon bidding farewell for the time being, I started walking out of the room feeling a sense of accomplishment. Suddenly, I heard Sophie say, "Max, Max come back." So I returned and she said, "Max, do you have a pen or pencil?"

"Yes," I replied.

She said, "Take down my address." This I did while saying to myself all along, "Well, what could she possibly want me to do with it? Visit her at some future date? Be invited over for a Friday evening Shabbat meal? Just what?"

I asked her, "Sophie, what do you want me to do with your address?"

She quickly and softly said, "Well your prayer was so wonderful, I want you to write it down, put it in an envelope and send it to God. I want to be sure he gets it and knows that it was given for me!" "*Shiken es tsu himl.*"—send it to heaven.

Such a Mentsh

Leo Roston defines *mentsh* as, "A human being, an upright honorable decent person. Someone of consequence, someone to admire and emulate, someone of noble character."

Isadore "Izzy" Crystal was the living embodiment of the word *mentsh*.

When I first met Isadore he was in his early eighties. Full of vitality and vigor, which he carried to his last days, Isadore spoke with a slight

Yiddish accent, actually eastern European. Words came out of his mouth as if they were emanating from an oyster bed of pearls, fresh from the bottom of the sea.

I don't think an unkind word was ever among them.

Always upbeat and positive, Isadore took a genuine interest in every one that he knew, whether the acquaintance stretched back sixty years or six hours—or for that matter, even if it had just begun. When he spoke to you, you automatically knew that you were tops on "Izzy's" list. He focused solely on you.

My relationship with Isadore extended over a period of years both on a social and business level. Regardless of when I saw him, it was always the same, "Hello Max, how are you? How is your Lillian, oy, what a doll? And what about your two brilliant lawyers, your son and such a wonderful daughter?"

Then he would say: "*Zug mir*? (Tell me/ What's new)." Regardless of how one felt, Izzy had that unique ability to make one feel that he or she was King or Queen of the hill. Once you left him, you had nothing but a good feeling about yourself and about life.

Thus, when he took ill, I was not at all surprised that upon visiting him at the hospital, his focus was on me. He had been ill for several months, but never once did he mention his own illness, nor did he ever become pre-occupied with it.

Before he slipped into a final coma, I visited him. On entering his room, I noticed his heavy breathing, which almost made it too difficult for him to speak. Yet when I told him to rest and say nothing, his immediate retort was: "Are you kidding? I have too much on my mind!"

"How is Lillian, Oy what a doll! Tell me about those brilliant lawyers of yours, your son and such a wonderful daughter?" We talked on for over an hour. He talked of his son, his daughters, and his many grandchildren, and his wife. He knew the end was near. Yet, not once did he mention his pain and illness.

He concluded our conversation by saying, "Max, let me tell you. Enjoy life, it is wonderful."

I looked at him and said, "Izzy, do you know that when God invented the word *mentsh*, God had you in mind." He looked up at me and simply said, "Max, I see you have learned." Such a *mentsh* was Izzy Crystal.

Tzedakeh

P roviding a caring community is at the heart of Jewish tradition. Three of the precepts that guide our community in extending love and support to individuals and families during difficult times are *Tzedakeh*—caring for the less fortunate through charitable gifts; *Gemilut Chasdim*—acts of loving kindness; and *Bikur Cholim*—visiting the sick.

One day while visiting at Abbot Northwestern Hospital, I ran into a fellow Temple Israel congregant who said to me, "Oh, Max, thank God you are here because Morris has just come out of open-heart surgery. He had two valves replaced and he is asking for a Rabbi. The family cannot seem to locate one. Please go to the cardiac ICU room and see them."

On arriving at the room, I sent in my card with the nurse. Two young women emerged. On seeing me, one of them said, "Oh, Rabbi, we are so glad to see you. Our father is crying out to see a Rabbi and he has been saying nothing else since coming through his surgery."

I explained that I was not a Rabbi, but merely a "para-rabbinic." I then told them that I would be honored to see their father.

On entering Morris's room, one of his daughters said, "Daddie, the Rabbi is here." I was standing at the end of the bed. Morris had nothing but tubes in him: tubes entering veins in his arms, tubes in his nose, tubes in his mouth.

I said, "Morris, I am here, what can I do for you?" Looking at me through the maze of tubes and a cold compress on his head, he somehow motioned to me with his hand to come closer. I moved to the center side of the bed. He motioned more for me to come even closer. On doing this, he gave one more gesture to move next to his mouth.

I said, "Morris, don't strain yourself. What can I do for you?" Morris, gasping to enunciate each word, said in a harsh garbled voice:

"Rabbi...Rabbi. Tell Abe Golden...tell Abe (a prominent member of our congregation and the community) ... please, tell Abe, I will make the pledge."

This would seem to be a fitting ending to the story. But it has two beautiful postscripts.

Several days later, after Morris recovered and returned home, I related the story to our Rabbi, Max Shapiro. On hearing the story, the Rabbi said, "Max, did you at least get him to sign the pledge card?"

But this was not the end of the story.

Two years later I met with Abe over lunch and related the story to him. He replied, "This is wonderful, now I can go see him and hit him up for a project I am working on, as I don't remember asking him for a pledge at that time."

That's *Tzedakeh*.

Mazel Tov!

How often can a ray of hope turn into a beacon of sunshine? This is especially true when someone enters the hospital thinking that he or she has very little hope of recovery. If such a patient does recover, it is usually considered the result of divine intervention—a miracle! Then there is the other alternative—finding that string that one can grab hold of—and like magic, one becomes a believer.

Such was the case with Eleanor, a lovely woman in her early seventies who had recently been diagnosed with an advanced state of colon cancer. Like many who learn that they have cancer, she had already given up all hope of recovery. To complicate matters, she had unbearable pain. On the afternoon that I saw her, she was being prepared for what had been described to her as "last minute surgery" on the very next morning.

Eleanor proceeded to tell me her life story. She embellished it with wonderful stories of her three grandchildren, the oldest of which was to be married in two months. Ever since the wedding date was set, Eleanor had dreamed of walking down the aisle with her husband, Nate. Once she was told of the cancer, her dreams of attending the wedding evaporated.

I asked Eleanor if I could share a story with her. By all means, she said. I proceeded to tell her about the time my wife and I went to visit our daughter who was attending Boston University. On our very first day, I came down with severe stomach pains. I had never experienced such pain before. We immediately made plans to return to Minneapolis.

On arriving back home, we went directly to see my internist, who informed me that I had gall stones. It would be necessary to have my gall bladder taken out. I was taken to Abbott Northwestern Hospital and prepared for surgery.

On being wheeled into the pre-op room, the anesthetist approached me and said, "Max, are you ready for me to put you out?"

I responded with a firm "No, I first want to talk to God."

He then relayed my response to my surgeon, who said "Max, may I listen in to your conversation with God?" I said Yes.

My talk to God went like this.

"God, I have been a pretty good guy all my life. Done wonderful things for people. Tried to live a righteous life and have been good to my family, my friends, and for that matter to mankind. Accordingly, I feel I have three blank checks with you. One of them I want to use today. The one I am cashing in says: I want to open my eyes within four hours after the surgery."

Sure enough, I did open my eyes within four hours.

Once I had relayed this story to Eleanor on the morning of her surgery, I looked at her and said, "Eleanor, I have two blank checks left. One

I am giving to you. So use it for whatever you wish!"

Tears started rolling down her cheeks. She said, "Really? How can you give me one?"

Four days later, I met with Eleanor as she was preparing to be discharged. She looked at me and said, "Do you know, Max, I used your blank check to ask that I come through my surgery and that my pain be gone so I can attend my granddaughter's wedding."

My response was a big smile followed by a hug. I simply said *Mazel Tov*.

Let me add one little postscript. Eleanor now has two great grandchildren.

Glossary

YIDDISH WORD	ENGLISH MEANING
Alevei	It should happen to me
Azoiner	Such a
Azoy Shein	How beautiful
Borekh	Thank (as with God)
Bashert	Meant to be; Destined
Bisel	Little
Es	It
Ess	Eat
Farblondzhet	Mixed up, confused
Fil	Lots of
Gan Eiden	Garden of Eden
Gemacht	Made
Gezunterheyt	In good health
Gut	Good
Hashe'm	God
Himl	Heaven
Kinder	Children
Loshen	Language
Maidel	Girl

Yiddish Word	English Meaning
Maivin	Expert
Malach	Angel
Mazel	Good fortune
Mazel Tov	Congratulations
Mazik	Mischievous boy
Mechaieh	Extreme pleasure
Main	My
Mentsh	A special person
Mitzva	Good work
Naches	Joy
Neshome	Soul, Spirit
Oy	Oh
Shaineh	Beautiful
Shiken	Send
Tsu	To
Tzedakeh	Charity
Vertashe'du	Do you speak
Vos	What
Zeigezunt	Be well

About the Author

Max Fallek was born in Albany, New York. He received a BA degree from the State University of New York in Albany and a MBA from the State University of Iowa. After serving in the United States Navy Reserve Office during the Korean War, Max started his business career with 3M, and was director of marketing for Tescom Corporation for 18 years. He was president and CEO of Quantum Group Food equipment mfr., and a marketing consultant from 1968 to 2003. He is the founder and past president of the American Institute of Small Business, a leading publisher of educational materials on entrepreneurship. Max himself wrote several books including *How to Set Up Your Own Small Business, How to Write a Business Plan,* and *Finding Money for Your Small Business.*

In recent years Max has been the Jewish Chaplain at Methodist Hospital and Minneapolis Veterans Home. he also makes Temple Israel congregant hospital calls.

Activities and Achievements:

Appointed by Presidents Reagan, Clinton, and Bush to serve on the National Advisory Council for Small Business.

Delegate of the White House Conference on Small Business.

Participated in the March on Washington.

Board member Temple Israel, Minneapolis, Aliveness Project, Minnesota School for the Blind (Former), Minnesota Symphonia, Neighborhood Involvement Program, Way Community Center, Minnesota Dance Company, Minneapolis Jewish Federation for Service, Past President of the Jewish Sheltering Home for Children (Orphanage), American Jewish Committee Midwest Chapter, 2001 Recipient of the Distinguished Alumni Award State University of New York at Albany.

Max and his wife Lillian's family includes son David, daughter Susan, and her husband Keith Grady.